UNVEILING THE MYSTERY OF THE RESURRECTION POWER

Johnson Akinfenwa

UNVEILING THE MYSTERY OF THE RESURRECTION POWER

ISBN-13: 978-1544890456

ISBN-10: 1544890451

Dedication

This book is dedicated to God the Father, the Son and the Holy Spirit who has anointed and bestowed the enabling grace over my life to write this book.

Therefore, I whole heartedly dedicate this book to the glory and honour of the everlasting kingdom of God.

MARANATHA!!!!

Contents

Acknowledgement

First and foremost, I want to acknowledge the Almighty God, the giver of my life. I give Him praise, honour, glory and adoration. I also give thanks to Jesus who enabled me to write and draw out the content of this book from the prophetic well of living water which he put inside of me. Praise and thanks to the Holy Spirit my great teacher and the source of my inspiration who endowed me with fresh revelation to write this book.

At this point, I will like to express my uncanny appreciation to my Apostolic Father, Dr Hugh Osgood of Charis Communication and the current president of the Free Churches in England and Wales. I owe the depth of my appreciation to him for taking his time to meticulously read through the manuscript of this book, guiding me through to ensure that the focus of this book is in line with the scripture and void of heresy. In addition to reading through he also took his time to write the foreword for the book as an expression of his endorsement that the book will bless the body of Christ globally. Thank you so much sir, and I pray that God will honour and increase his anointing upon you, with good health and long life.

Also, my immense thanks to my wonderful daughter Charissa Ibiyemi Akinfenwa for her support by sacrificing some of her time in typing the manuscript in preparation for publication. Thank you and God bless you daughter.

Finally, my heartfelt thanks to my beloved wife, Pastor Funmi Akinfenwa for her encouragement, support, suggestion and her patience which helps me to concentrate on writing this book. In the same way, I will like to appreciate my sons- Emmanuel and Israel Akinfenwa whose words of encouragement and support served as a source of inspiration to complete this book writing project. Also, I would like to appreciate my wonderful daughters Daiella, Charissa and Irene Grace. I give praise to God for such a wonderful family that God has surrounded me with, especially my wife and our thoughtful children who believed with me and in me as a covenant servant of God.

Foreword

In this book, the first in a three-part series, Johnson Akinfenwa not only focuses on the power that God invested in the resurrection but highlights the benefits for us that emanate from it. There is no doubt that the cross and resurrection stand together as the pivotal point of human history, and it behoves us to delve more deeply into the transformation that such a demonstration of God's power has accomplished historically in readiness for us to appropriate spiritually.

In introducing this book, I also want to signal up the pattern that develops across the series. As it looks first at the power of the resurrection, and then at the power in the blood of the cross, a picture is being built up of the authority that God intends us, as Christian believers, to exhibit in our day-to-day lives. This authority is the subject of the third book.

Those who are familiar with the emphases that mark my own ministry will know that I firmly believe that such authority must always go hand-in-hand with humility. Furthermore, it is well known that I also have an aversion to any teaching that seeks to put us on a par with the Almighty. Nevertheless, as humility and authority were never intended to be alternative options, I am well aware that the Church can lack both, so this book comes as a timely challenge. We do need to be a truly resurrection-empowered Church, walking in humility yet raised up under the mighty hand of God.

My hope is that as you read this book you will be stimulated to think afresh about '*the exceeding greatness of His power towards us who believe, according to the working of His mighty power which He worked in Christ when He raised Him from the dead and seated Him at His right hand in the heavenly places, far above all principality and power and might and dominion and every name that is named, not only in the age but in that which is to come'.* (Ephesians 1:19-21).

Thank you, Johnson, for writing this trilogy.

Hugh Osgood
March 2017

Chapter One
INTRODUCTION

That I may know him, and the power of his resurrection… (Philippians 3:10)

As we can see from the above quotation, one of the most passionate prayers of the Apostle Paul was to have a full knowledge of the power of Christ's resurrection. Yet, until today, the topic of resurrection power remains one of the most profound mysteries of the Bible. The understanding of it is progressive and based upon the degree of fresh revelation brought to the Church in every dispensation from the days of the apostles until now.

The Apostle Paul also made it clear in the book of Ephesians that in every dispensation the apostles and the prophets are the custodians (trustees) of the mystery of the revelation knowledge of Christ:

How that by revelation he made known unto me the mystery; (as I wrote afore in few words, whereby, when ye read, ye may understand my knowledge in the mystery of Christ) which in other ages was not made known unto the sons of men, as it is now revealed unto his holy apostles and prophets by the Spirit. (Ephesians 3:3-5)

The fresh revelation of the mystery of the knowledge of God is downloaded into the hearts of the prophets and the apostles by the Holy Spirit. This is then revealed to the Body of Christ through their apostolic and prophetic teachings or doctrines.

The secret things belong to the LORD our God, but the things which are revealed *and* disclosed belong to us and to our children forever, so that we may do all of the words of this law. (Deuteronomy 29:29)

The mystery embedded in the power of resurrection is so enormous, and the understanding of it is so deep, that although God through the inspiration of the Holy Spirit, gave much revelation on this topic to Apostle Paul, Paul himself declared that we cannot know everything about this mystery all at once. God's mercies are new every morning and His ways are unsearchable so that we only know in part:

O the depth of the riches both of the wisdom and knowledge of God! how unsearchable are his judgments, and his ways past finding out!. (Romans 11:33)

For we know in part, and we prophesy in part. (1 Corinthians 13:9)

I believe the reason why God reveals the mystery of His word to us little by little is so that every part of His revelation moves us, individually or corporately, from one realm of glory to another.

But we all, with open face beholding as in a glass the glory of the Lord, are changed into the same image from glory to glory, even as by the Spirit of the Lord. (2 Corinthians 3:18)

The words of God fashion us daily as believers to be conformed to the image and the likeness of God in Christ. Every day we graduate from one level of glory to another until Christ is fully revealed in us.

Till we all come in the unity of the faith, and of the knowledge of the Son of God, unto a perfect man, unto the measure of the stature of the fulness of Christ: (Ephesians 4:13)

WORD OF WISDOM

The revelation of the glory of God given yesterday is not sufficient to reveal the glory of God for today. However, the revelation of God's glory given yesterday is a recipe for today's revealed glory. Hence, the revelation of today is embedded in the one revealed yesterday. (Prophet Johnson Akinfenwa).

It is my prayer that God through the power of the Holy Spirit will impact us with this fresh revelation regarding resurrection power. I also pray that the understanding of the enormous power embedded in the mystery of the resurrection will move the entire Body of Christ to the next level of God's glory, so as to affect and influence our generation for Jesus Christ. Amen!

Chapter Two
UNDERSTANDING RESURRECTION POWER

After Jesus had risen from the dead by resurrection power, He lived on the earth for another forty days, during which time He showed Himself to about 500 disciples. After forty days, before He ascended to heaven, He commissioned His disciples by giving them all authority and power to govern and rule the world. The authority and power that He gave to them (the Church) was the invincible power of His resurrection. This is the power that raised Him from the dead and made Him the ruler of the heavens, the earth and all that is underneath the earth.

For this reason I would like to bring to your attention the scripture references below:

And being found in fashion as a man, he humbled himself, and became obedient unto death, even the death of the cross.

Wherefore God also hath highly exalted him, and given him a name which is above every name: That at the name of Jesus every knee should bow, of things in heaven, and things in earth, and things under the earth; And that every tongue should confess that Jesus Christ is Lord, to the glory of God the Father. (Philippians 2:8-11)

Know ye not, that so many of us as were baptized into Jesus Christ were baptized into his death? Therefore we are buried with him by baptism into death: that like as Christ was raised up from the dead by the glory of the Father, even so we also should walk in

newness of life. For if we have been planted together in the likeness of his death, we shall be also in the likeness of his resurrection: (Romans 6:3-5)

But if the Spirit of him that raised up Jesus from the dead dwell in you, he that raised up Christ from the dead shall also quicken your mortal bodies by his Spirit that dwelleth in you. (Romans 8:11)

In these scriptures, some phrases stand out, namely that the Holy Spirit is the Spirit of resurrection and of glory.

It was in the power of the resurrection that Jesus commissioned His Church to go and influence the world with the gospel. This power, therefore, bestowed on us the capacity to operate in the supernatural, making the Church become an invincible force on this planet earth.

Now unto him that is able to do exceeding abundantly above all that we ask or think, according to the power that worketh in us, (Ephesians 3:20)

This is the power that makes us to be EXTRAORDINARY even though we are ORDINARY. This power awards us the OBE...Ordinary But Extraordinary.

The resurrection of Jesus from the dead through the power of the Holy Spirit represents the most outstanding evidence of the accomplished work of redemption. It is this same power of resurrection that bestowed upon the Church an immeasurable dominion authority and power to govern the earth and exercise authority over the kingdom of darkness ruled by Satan and all his demons._The Church (the body of Christ) thus becomes the embodiment of the totality of the power of the resurrected Jesus. Christ

Himself is the Head of His blood-bought triumphant Church.

And hath put all things under his feet, and gave him to be the head over all things to the church, which is his body, the fulness of him that filleth all in all (Ephesians 1: 22-23)

Furthermore, resurrection authority and power liberated the Adamic (human) race from the oppression and the imprisonment of Satan. Through the accomplished work of Calvary, by the shedding of the blood of Jesus, we became sons of God (a new set of people), with elevated status far beyond the status of the first Adam. How? We have the answer in Ephesians 2:4-6:

But God, who is rich in mercy, for his great love wherewith he loved us, even when we were dead in sins, hath quickened us together with Christ, (by grace ye are saved;) and hath raised us

up together, and made us sit together in heavenly places in Christ Jesus:

In the next chapter I will explain further the mystery and the power of resurrection based upon the text above.

Chapter Three
THE MYSTERY OF RESURRECTION POWER

The understanding of the mystery of the Word of God is given by the inspiration of the Holy Spirit. Furthermore, according to Ephesians 3:3-5, Deuteronomy 29:29 and 1 Corinthians 4:1, God has given us (believers) the privilege to be the custodians of the mystery of the revelation of God's Word:

The secret things belong to the LORD our God, but the things which are revealed *and* disclosed belong to us and to our children forever, so that we may do all of the words of this law. (2 Chronicles 29:29.)

How that by revelation he made known unto me the mystery; (as I wrote afore in few words, whereby, when ye read, ye may understand my knowledge in the mystery of Christ) which in other ages was not made known unto the sons of men, as it is now revealed unto his holy apostles and prophets by the Spirit; (Ephesians 3:3-5)

Let a man so account of us, as of the ministers of Christ, and stewards of the mysteries of God. (1 Corinthians 4:1.)

On this note I would like to explain the mystery of resurrection power as the Holy Spirit revealed it to me based on the content of Ephesians 2: 4-6.

But God, who is rich in mercy, for his great love wherewith he loved us, even when we were dead in sins, hath quickened us together with Christ, (by grace ye are saved;) and hath raised us up together, and made us sit together in heavenly places in Christ Jesus:

A critical examination of the above scripture reveals that the operation of resurrection power consists of two realms:

1. **Transformational (quickening) resurrection power**
2. **Translational (Ascension) resurrection power**

Each of these dimensions of power will be explained in the subsequent chapters.

Chapter Four

TRANSFORMATIONAL RESURRECTION POWER

The word transformation, according to the thesaurus, means a radical change or alteration. It also means "metamorphosis", "renewal" or "transfiguration". Each of these meanings highlights what transformational resurrection power is all about.

The first evidence of transformational resurrection power was demonstrated on earth when Jesus raised Lazarus from the dead. This whole story is in the eleventh chapter of the Gospel according to St John. In this chapter Jesus demonstrated that He is the embodiment of resurrection power.

Then said Martha unto Jesus, Lord, if thou hadst been here, my brother had not died. But I know, that even now, whatsoever thou wilt ask of God, God will give it thee. Jesus saith unto her, Thy brother shall rise again. Martha saith unto him, I know that he shall rise again in the resurrection at the last day. Jesus said unto her, I am the resurrection, and the life: he that believeth in me, though he were dead, yet shall he live. (John 11:21-25)

On the occasion when Lazarus died, Jesus was away. In fact, when Jesus arrived, Lazarus had been buried four days, with his sepulchre covered with a heavy stone... Lazarus was already stinking!

Jesus therefore again groaning in himself cometh to the grave. It was a cave, and a stone lay upon it. Jesus said, Take ye away the stone. Martha, the sister of him that was dead, saith unto him, Lord, by this time he stinketh: for he hath been dead four days. Jesus saith unto her, Said I not unto thee, that, if thou wouldest believe, thou shouldest see the glory of God? Then they took away the stone from the place where the dead was laid. And Jesus lifted up his eyes, and said, Father, I thank thee that thou hast heard me. And I knew that thou hearest me always: but because of the people which stand by I said it, that they may believe that thou hast sent me. And when he thus had spoken, he cried with a loud voice, Lazarus, come forth. And he that was dead came forth, bound hand and foot with graveclothes: and his face was bound

about with a napkin. Jesus saith unto them, Loose him, and let him go. Then many of the Jews which came to Mary, and had seen the things which Jesus did, believed on him. (John 11:38-45)

In these verses there is a powerful revelation of the real definition of resurrection power.

Definition: Resurrection power can be defined as: 'the supernatural demonstration and the manifestation of the glory of God in a matter, issues or problem that is naturally impossible for man to solve'.

By raising Lazarus from the dead, Jesus demonstrated to the world that He has power over death and that He is truly the resurrection and the life. It is not surprising then that the Bible says even death could not hold Jesus captive...Hallelujah!

The pinnacle of resurrection power was revealed after Jesus Christ Himself was crucified, buried and rose again on the third day. The stone at the mouth of the sepulchre was rolled away and the risen Lord was free. This is the transformational (quickening) power that brought the body of Jesus from death back to life, even after He had stayed for three days in the belly of the earth. All this happened because Jesus, according to the book of Revelation, has the keys of death and hell.

I am he that liveth, and was dead; and, behold, I am alive for evermore, Amen; and have the keys of hell and of death. (Revelation 1:18)

Whom God hath raised up, having loosed the pains of death: because it was not possible that he should be holden of it. (Acts 2:24)

In Christ coming back to life after three days the Holy Spirit has shown me that three major principalities were conquered. These are **Death, Corruption** and **the Grave.**

And when the Sabbath was past, Mary Magdalene, and Mary the mother of James, and Salome, had bought sweet spices, that they might come and anoint him. And very early in the morning the first day of the week, they came unto the sepulchre at the rising of the sun. And they said among themselves, Who shall roll us away the stone from the door of the sepulchre? And when they looked, they saw that the stone was rolled away: for it was very great. (Mark 16:1-4)

How did Jesus come alive from the grave when barricaded in with a heavy stone? The answer is that it is impossible for death or a heavy stone to hold him captive. His resurrection from the dead was the fulfilment of a prophecy given through King David in the book of Psalms:

I have set the Lord always before me: because he is at my right hand, I shall not be moved. Therefore my heart is glad, and my glory rejoiceth: my flesh also shall rest in hope. For thou wilt not leave my soul in hell; neither wilt thou suffer thine Holy One to see corruption. (Psalm 16:8-10)

It was not a coincidence that the Apostle Peter made a reference to the above prophecy on the day of Pentecost in order to expose the ignorance of the Jews that were present. He made them realise that the resurrection of Jesus Christ was exactly what their prophet had predicted many centuries before.

This Jesus, when delivered up according to the definite and fixed purpose and settled plan and foreknowledge of God, you crucified and put out of the way [killing Him] by the hands of lawless and wicked men [But] God raised Him up, liberating Him from the pangs of death, seeing that it was not possible for Him to continue to be controlled or retained by it. I saw the Lord always before me. Because he is at my right hand, I will not be shaken. Therefore my heart is glad and my tongue rejoices; my body also will rest in hope, because you will not abandon me to the realm of the dead, you will not let your holy one see decay. (Acts 2: 23-27 AMP)

The Bible tells us that when we were dead in sins, the resurrection power quickened us (it brought us from death to life) together with Christ' (Ephesians 2:5). This represents the total defeat of all forms of the works of the flesh which result in sin and death as written in Galatians 5:19-21.

Another interesting scripture given to us by Apostle Paul in his epistle to the Galatians reveals to us that when Jesus was crucified, we were crucified with Him and came alive with Him so that He lives in us. All of this happened through the power of the resurrection.

I am crucified with Christ: nevertheless I live; yet not I, but Christ liveth in me: and the life which I now live in the flesh I live by the faith of the Son of God, who loved me, and gave himself for me. (Galatians. 2: 20).

Paul was telling believers that when Jesus was nailed to the cross all the works of the flesh (the nature of sin) were nailed there together with Him, and when Jesus rose from the dead we rose with Him with a new life and as a new creation. This mystery (transformational resurrection power) is elucidated further in the epistle to the Corinthian church:

...and He died for all, so that all those who live would no longer live for themselves, but for Him who died and was raised for their sake. So from now on we regard no one from a human point of view [according to worldly standards and values]. Though we have known Christ from a human point of view, now we no longer know Him in this way. Therefore if anyone is in Christ [that is, grafted in, joined to Him by faith in Him as Saviour], he is a new creature [reborn and renewed by the Holy Spirit]; the old things [the previous moral and spiritual condition] have passed away. Behold, new things have come [because spiritual awakening brings a new life.] (2 Corinthians 5:15-17 AMP).

Furthermore, when we examine the mystery of resurrection power in relation to Ephesians 2:6 it tells us that we were quickened together with Christ from death to life. This happened through transformational supernatural resurrection power. This power bestowed supernatural authority upon every believer to exercise dominion over **death**, **corruption** and **the grave**. The assignment of these three principal agents of Satan against every human being is to kill, steal and destroy.

The thief comes only in order to steal and kill and destroy. I came that they may have and enjoy life, and have it in abundance (to the full, till it overflows). (John 10: 9-10)

Praise God, the law of the Spirit of life in Christ gave us power over these three principal demons according to Romans 8: 1-3:

There is therefore now no condemnation to them which are in Christ Jesus, who walk not after the flesh, but after the Spirit. For the law of the Spirit of life in Christ Jesus hath made me free from the law of sin and death. For what the law could not do, in that it was weak through the flesh, God sending his own Son in the likeness of sinful flesh, and for sin, condemned sin in the flesh:

But God shows and clearly proves His [own] love for us by the fact that while we were still sinners, Christ (the Messiah, the Anointed One) died for us. Therefore, since we are now justified (acquitted, made righteous, and brought into right relationship with God) by Christ's blood, how much more [certain is it that] we shall be saved by Him from the indignation and wrath of God. For if while we were

enemies we were reconciled to God through the death of His Son, it is much more [certain], now that we are reconciled, that we shall be saved (daily delivered from sin's dominion) through His [resurrection] life. (Romans 5:8-10 AMP.)

Praise God! By the power of resurrection I have overcome **death**, **corruption** and **the grave**...marked by the blood of Jesus. Hallelujah! Also by His grace I have been given authority and power to raise the dead... as partaker of His glory of resurrection.

And as ye go, preach, saying, The kingdom of heaven is at hand. Heal the sick, cleanse the lepers, raise the dead, cast out devils: freely ye have received, freely give. (Matthew 10:7-8)

Chapter Five
TRANSLATIONAL RESURRECTION POWER

According to Collins Dictionary, translation means ‘to transfer (a person) from one place or position to another’. Another definition of translation says ‘the transfer of a person from one place or plane of existence to another, as from the earth to heaven’. This definition perfectly fits into the translation (ascension) of Jesus Christ from the earth to heaven.

Therefore the translational (ascension) resurrection power is the supernatural power that lifted up (translated) Jesus from the earthly realm to the heavenly.

Through this power we too ascended by faith to heaven in Christ to sit with Christ in God’s presence and it is in this power, and from this heavenly positioning, that we can establish God's Kingdom rule and enforce His kingdom dominion authority over the power of darkness. In this way we are able to enforce the will of God on the earth. Although, the church is yet to come to the fullness of the revelation of this resurrection power that is made available to us, it is this immeasurable power that forms the basis of the prayer of the Apostle Paul to the Ephesians:

That the God of our Lord Jesus Christ, the Father of glory, may give unto you the spirit of wisdom and revelation in the knowledge of him: The eyes of your understanding being enlightened; that ye may know what is the hope of his calling, and what the riches of the glory of his inheritance in the saints, And what is the exceeding greatness of his power to us-ward who believe, according to the working of his mighty

power, Which he wrought in Christ, when he raised him from the dead, and set him at his own right hand in the heavenly places, Far above all principality, and power, and might, and dominion, and every name that is named, not only in this world, but also in that which is to come. (Ephesians 1:17-21)

The underlined phrase in the above text, points to the two dimensional realms of resurrection power, namely: Transformational Resurrection Power ('...when he raised him from the dead...') and Translational Resurrection Power *('...and set him at his own right hand in the heavenly places*').

The operation of these two realms of resurrection power is what delivered us from the kingdom of Satan. That is to say that we were delivered from the activities of the wicked human agents and the demon spirits, and elevated to our status of being seated in heavenly places with Christ. This fact is highlighted in Colossians 1:12-13.

Giving thanks unto the Father, which hath made us meet to be partakers of the inheritance of the saints in light: Who hath delivered us from the power of darkness, and hath translated us into the kingdom of his dear Son:

Through the ascension power, we ascended together with Jesus, leading captivity captive to fulfil the prophecy in Psalm 68:18-19 in order to take back the gifts Satan stole from the first Adam.

Thou hast ascended on high, thou hast led captivity captive: thou hast received gifts for men; yea, for the rebellious also, that the Lord God might dwell among them. Blessed be the Lord, who daily loadeth us with benefits, even the God of our salvation. Selah.

Satan took humanity out of God's presence and stole the fullness of the royalty and dominion authority that was due to humanity as kings on the earth. (Genesis 1:26-28). This happened when Adam fell through the deception of Satan.

What is the fullness of our royalty? The fullness of our royalty (as believers) is entrenched in the fact that we were made in the image of God with the ability to be exactly His true expression and to govern the earth by the creative power of the word of our mouth. This means that we were made originally as the sons of God with dominion authority. This is stated in Genesis 1:26-28:

And God said, Let us make man in our image, after our likeness: and let them have dominion over the fish of the sea, and over the fowl of the air, and over the cattle, and over all the earth, and over every creeping thing that creepeth upon the earth. So God created man in his own image, in the image of God created he him; male and female created he them. And God blessed them, and God said unto them, Be fruitful, and multiply, and replenish the earth, and subdue it: and have dominion over the fish of the sea, and over the fowl of the air, and over every living thing that moveth upon the earth.

PRAYER: In the name of Jesus and by the power of the Holy Spirit I receive revelation knowledge to understand the mystery of the power of resurrection and its application to live a victorious life. In Jesus name. Amen!

Chapter Six

RESTORING OUR STATUS AS SONS OF GOD

The reason why Jesus came was to restore us to humanity's original status as the true expression of God's image. But equally true is the fact that believers have a higher dominion authority and power than the first Adam. This means that His death and resurrection has produced a new set of people, known as the sons of God, in fulfilment of Psalm 2:7-8:

I will declare the decree: the Lord hath said unto me, Thou art my Son; this day have I begotten thee. Ask of me, and I shall give thee the heathen for thine inheritance, and the uttermost parts of the earth for thy possession.

Jesus was empowered with the Holy Spirit at His baptism in order that we might through Him become sons of God with power:

And Jesus, when he was baptized, went up straightway out of the water: and, lo, the heavens were opened unto him, and he saw the Spirit of God descending like a dove, and lighting upon him: And lo a voice from heaven, saying, This is my beloved Son, in whom I am well pleased. (Matthew 3:16-17)

As a result of the above, whosoever believes Jesus is the son of God becomes a son of God and a partaker of the power of God, receiving the Holy Spirit. This is the assertion of John 1:12:

But as many as received him, to them gave he power to become the sons of God, even to them that believe on his name.

Further scriptures below exemplify the fact that not only is Jesus the Son of God with power but we are sons of God with power too:

God, who at sundry times and in divers manners spake in time past unto the fathers by the prophets, Hath in these last days spoken unto us by his Son, whom he hath appointed heir of all things, by whom also he made the worlds; <u>Who being the brightness of his glory, and the express image of his person,</u> and upholding all things by the word of his power, when he had by himself purged our sins, sat down on

the right hand of the Majesty on high. (Hebrews 1:1-3)

Concerning his Son Jesus Christ our Lord, which was made of the seed of David according to the flesh and declared to be the Son of God with power, according to the spirit of holiness, by the resurrection from the dead: (Romans 1:3-4)

In order to secure the status of sonship for us, and to have us fully identify with Him, this is what Jesus went through according to the epistle to the Hebrews:

But we see Jesus, who was made a little lower than the angels for the suffering of death, crowned with glory and honour; that he by the grace of God should taste death for every man. For it became him, for whom are all things, and by whom are all things, in bringing many sons unto glory, to make the captain of their salvation perfect through sufferings. For both he that sanctifieth and they who are sanctified are all of one: for which cause he is not ashamed to call them brethren, Saying, I will declare thy name unto my brethren, in the midst of the church will I sing praise unto thee. (Hebrews 2:9-12)

This is the reason why the Bible says we are complete in Him as the Church becomes the fullness of God in Christ.

And ye are complete in him, which is the head of all principality and power: (Colossians 2:10)

I want to categorically state here that the evidence of our sonship with God is the fact that we have been empowered, equipped by the Spirit of God, and most importantly that we are being led by the Spirit of God the Father:

For as many as are led by the Spirit of God, they are the sons of God. For ye have not received the spirit of bondage again to fear; but ye have received the Spirit of adoption, whereby we cry, Abba, Father. The Spirit itself beareth witness with our spirit, that we are the children of God. (Romans 8:14-16)

The climax of our redemption in Christ is His presentation of us, the Church, to God as a kingdom of priests and kings. It is His heavenly positioning that gives us the full capacity to reign and govern the earth with dominion authority over principalities and powers.

In seeing ourselves as those who have ascended with Christ, we share in His ascension. On that ascension day there was a great ceremony in the heavens and the heavenly hosts will also welcome us in full royal regalia, heralding us into God's presence with a triumphant song of victory from the angelic hosts. On that day, I believe that each believer will be decorated with **seven royal signets** which are ...power, riches, wisdom, strength, honour, glory and blessings which we will carry as a tribute to Christ.

And hast made us unto our God kings and priests: and we shall reign on the earth. And I beheld, and I heard the voice of many angels round about the throne and the beasts and the elders: and the number of them was ten thousand times ten thousand, and thousands of thousands; Saying with a loud voice, Worthy is the Lamb that was slain to receive power, and riches, and wisdom, and strength, and honour, and glory, and blessing. (Revelation 5:10-12)

The day of our triumphant entry to heaven is also described in Hebrews 12:22-24.

But ye are come unto mount Sion, and unto the city of the living God, the heavenly Jerusalem, and to an innumerable company of angels, To the general assembly and church of the firstborn, which are written in heaven, and to God the Judge of all, and to the spirits of just men made perfect, And to Jesus the mediator of the new covenant, and to the blood of sprinkling, that speaketh better things than that of Abel.

In coming to the general assembly and Church of the Firstborn, it could be said that we become members of a heavenly parliament. This will be explained further in the next chapter.

Chapter Seven
SECURING OUR MEMBERSHIP OF THE HEAVENLY PARLIAMENT

When the Bible says that we are seated together with Christ in the heavenly places (Ephesians 2:6), to me this implies that every believer is a member of a heavenly parliament. It is also interesting to notice that members of the earthly House of Parliament carry out their deliberations while sitting. Each of them holds an equal seat and carries equal voting power. By implication we have equal seats, equal voting right and equal veto power in the heavenly parliament, being positioned alongside Christ as sons.

We have joint legislative power with God the Father, Jesus and the Holy Spirit to decree and to enforce dominion authority so as to establish the will of God over the earth. We have this privilege because believers have been declared as the members of a heavenly general assembly by the virtue of the work of redemption through the shed blood of Jesus. Let us consider again Hebrews 12: 22-24:

But ye are come unto mount Sion, and unto the city of the living God, the heavenly Jerusalem, and to an innumerable company of angels to the general assembly and church of the firstborn, which are written in heaven, and to God the Judge of all, and to the spirits of just men made perfect, and to Jesus the mediator of the new covenant, and to the blood of sprinkling, that speaketh better things than that of Abel. See that ye refuse not him that speaketh. For if they escaped not who refused him that spake on earth, much more shall not

we escape, if we turn away from him that speaketh from heaven.

Everything in Mount Zion, the heavenly parliament, is controlled from God's throne of grace, which is the New Testament equivalent of the Mercy Seat and is the parallel to the Speaker's chair in an earthly Parliament.

It seems from the above quotation that the blood of Jesus is the 'Speaker of the House', confirming that the function of the blood has not changed since the Old Testament. God always spoke through the blood on the Mercy Seat.

And all the oxen for the sacrifice of the peace offerings were twenty and four bullocks, the rams sixty, the he goats sixty, the lambs of the first year sixty. This was the dedication of the altar, after that it was anointed.

And when Moses was gone into the tabernacle of the congregation to speak with him, then he heard the voice of one speaking unto him from off the mercy seat that was upon the ark of testimony, from between the two cherubims: and he spake unto him. (Number 7:88-89)

PRAYER: In Jesus name, I pray that the blood will speak abundant blessings protection, and uncommon favour over your live and your family. Let the BLOOD speak! Amen.

Chapter 8

GAINING DOMINION OVER DEATH

But we see Jesus, who was made a little lower than the angels for the suffering of death, crowned with glory and honour; that he by the grace of God should taste death for every man. For it became him, for whom are all things, and by whom are all things, in bringing many sons unto glory, to make the captain of their salvation perfect through sufferings. For both he that sanctifieth and they who are sanctified are all of one: for which cause he is not ashamed to call them brethren, Saying, I will declare thy name unto my brethren, in the midst of the church will I sing praise unto thee. And again, I will put my trust in him. And again, Behold I and the children which God hath given me.

Forasmuch then as the children are partakers of flesh and blood, he also himself likewise took part of the same; that through death he might destroy him that had the power of death, that is, the devil; and deliver them who through fear of death were all their lifetime subject to bondage. (Hebrews 2:9-15)

The above scripture implies that through Christ's identification with us we can claim a legitimate authority to enforce God's will on the earth and to establish His Kingdom as we thwart the operations of the devil with the help of a multitude of angels. Further evidence that the rulership of the earth has been entrusted to man is afforded by the following scriptures:

When I consider thy heavens, the work of thy fingers, the moon and the stars, which thou hast ordained; What is man, that thou art mindful of him? and the son of man, that thou visitest him? For thou hast made him a little lower than the angels, and hast crowned him with glory and honour. Thou madest him to have dominion over the works of thy hands; thou hast put all things under his feet: (Psalm 8:3-6)

But the saints of the most High shall take the kingdom, and possess the kingdom for ever, even for ever and ever...And the kingdom and dominion, and the greatness of the kingdom under the whole heaven, shall be given to the people of the saints of the most High, whose kingdom is an everlasting kingdom, and all dominions shall serve and obey him. (Daniel 7:18 & 27)

Daniel's revelation relates to the new world to come and confirms that God intends every believer to rule and to take dominion after the second coming of Christ Jesus. Thus, our responsibility as believers is to rise into action and by faith in Christ to administer the earth by enforcing the **will** and **purpose** of God through the power of His words, His blood and His Spirit.(1John 5:8).

Chapter Nine

HAVING THE RIGHT TO ENFORCE GOD'S WILL ON EARTH

Our ability to enforce the will of God on earth comes from our heavenly positioning:

Among whom also we all had our conversation in times past in the lusts of our flesh, fulfilling the desires of the flesh and of the mind; and were by nature the children of wrath, even as others. But God, who is rich in mercy, for his great love wherewith he loved us, even when we were dead in sins, hath quickened us together with Christ, (by grace ye are saved); and hath raised us up together, and made us sit together in heavenly places in Christ Jesus: (Ephesians 2:3-6)

Through deeper understanding by the inspiration of the Holy Spirit, four truths stand out from the above verses. These are:

- Believers have equal POWER with Christ to do greater exploit:

Verily, verily, I say unto you, He that believeth on me, the works that I do shall he do also; and greater works than these shall he do; because I go unto my Father. (John 14:12)

- Believers have equal POSITION with Christ:

And hath raised us up together, and made us sit together in heavenly places in Christ Jesus: (Ephesians 2:6)

- Believers have equal POSSESSION with Christ:

Even so we, when we were children, were in bondage under the elements of the world: but when the fulness of the time was come, God sent forth his Son, made of a woman, made under the law, to redeem them that were under the law, that we might receive the adoption of sons. And because ye are sons, God hath sent forth the Spirit of his Son into your hearts, crying, Abba, Father. Wherefore thou art no more a servant, but a son; and if a son, then an heir of God through Christ. (Galatians 4:3-7)

- Believers have equal SONSHIP STATUS(PATERNITY) with Christ:

But we see Jesus, who was made a little lower than the angels for the suffering of death, crowned with glory and honour; that he by the grace of God should taste death for every man. For it became him, for whom are all things, and by whom are all things, in bringing many sons unto glory, to make the captain of their salvation perfect through sufferings. For both he that sanctifieth and they who are sanctified are all of one: for which cause he is not ashamed to call them brethren, Saying, I will declare thy name unto my brethren, in the midst of the church will I sing praise unto thee. (Hebrews 2:9-12.)

We will now examine some additional scriptures to further establish the fact that we have been given authority and power to enforce and establish the Kingdom of God on the earth, by casting out demons and destroying the works of the devil.

PRAYING DOWN THE KINGDOM

For the kingdom is the LORD'S: and he is the governor among the nations. (Psalm 22:28)

After this manner therefore pray ye: Our Father which art in heaven, Hallowed be thy name. Thy kingdom come, Thy will be done in earth, as it is in heaven. (Matthew 6:9-10)

For the kingdom of God is not in word, but in power. (1Corinthians 4:20-21)

PREACHING AND DEMONSTRATING KINGDOM POWER

And when he had called unto him his twelve disciples, he gave them power against unclean spirits, to cast them out, and to heal all manner of sickness and all manner of disease. (Matthew 10:1)

And as ye go, preach, saying, The kingdom of heaven is at hand. Heal the sick, cleanse the lepers, raise the dead, cast out devils: freely ye have received, freely give." (Matthew 10:7-8)

For the kingdom of God is not in word, but in power. (1Corinthians 4:20-21)

ENFORCING AND EXECUTING KINGDOM POWER BY THE AUTHORITY OF GOD'S WORD

Verily I say unto you, Whatsoever ye shall bind on earth shall be bound in heaven: and whatsoever ye shall loose on earth shall be loosed in heaven. (Matthew 18:18)

Acquaint now thyself with him, and be at peace: thereby good shall come unto thee. Receive, I pray thee, the law from his mouth, and lay up his words in thine heart. Thou shalt also decree a thing, and it shall be established unto thee: and the light shall shine upon thy ways. (Job 22:21-22 & 28)

Let the high praises of God be in their mouth, and a two-edged sword in their hand; To execute vengeance upon the heathen, and punishments upon the people; To bind their kings with chains, and their nobles with fetters of iron; To execute upon them the judgment written: this honour have all his saints. Praise ye the Lord. (Psalm 149:6-9)

And Jesus came and spake unto them, saying, All power is given unto me in heaven and in earth. Go ye therefore, and teach all nations, baptizing them in the name of the Father, and of the Son, and of the Holy Ghost: Teaching them to observe all things whatsoever I have commanded you: and, lo, I am with you always, even unto the end of the world. Amen. (Matthew 28:18-20)

These scriptures show that Christians have been given invincible, ever-conquering and triumphant resurrection power in order to establish the Kingdom of God on the earth. This is the task that must be completed by the end of the Church Age.

Chapter Ten
CONQUERING DEATH, CORRUPTION AND THE GRAVE

Resurrection power gives us victory over the principal demons of **death**, **corruption** and **the grave**.

These three principal demons work for Satan against human beings, whether believers or non-believers. One does not need to die in order to experience the evil effect of these three demons on a daily basis. They can manifest in different spheres of human activity, e.g. business, marriage, bodily sickness, ministries, relationships and many other areas of human life. The assignment of these demons is to kill, steal and destroy.

But glory be to God! Jesus made a profound statement to reveal how He will deal with these three principal satanic forces.

The thief cometh not, but for to steal, and to kill, and to destroy: I am come that they might have life, and that they might have it more abundantly. (John 10:10)

In fact, when Jesus was hanging on the cross, even as His blood touched the ground, **death**, **corruption** and **the grave**, together with every religious spirit were instantaneously defeated. Hallelujah! This fact can be found in Matthew 27:50-55:

Jesus, when he had cried again with a loud voice, yielded up the ghost. And, behold, the veil of the temple was rent in twain from the top to the bottom; and the earth did quake, and the rocks rent; and the graves were opened; and many bodies of the saints which slept arose, and came out of the graves after his resurrection, and went into the holy city, and appeared unto many.

Now when the centurion, and they that were with him, watching Jesus, saw the earthquake, and those things that were done, they feared greatly, saying, Truly this was the Son of God. And many women were there beholding afar off, which followed Jesus from Galilee, ministering unto him.

And when Jesus rose from the dead, He affirmed with evidence that all power over death, corruption and the grave has been given to Him, in heaven, on the earth and under the earth.

And Jesus came and spake unto them, saying, All power is given unto me in heaven and in earth. (Matthew 28:18)

Furthermore, God has given Jesus a name far above every other name, both in heaven or on the earth:

And being found in fashion as a man, he humbled himself, and became obedient unto death, even the death of the cross. Wherefore God also hath highly exalted him, and given him a name which is above every name: That at the name of Jesus every knee should bow, of things in heaven, and things in earth, and things under the earth; (Philippians 2:8-10)

We need to note the three major realms mentioned in these verses: the heavens, the earth, and under the earth. We shall return to them shortly.

Meanwhile we continue to affirm that **once death is defeated, sin is powerless and the grave is jobless. Amen!**

O death, where is thy sting? O grave, where is thy victory? The sting of death is sin; and the strength of sin is the law. But thanks be to God, which giveth us the victory through our Lord Jesus Christ. (1 Corinthians 15:55-57)

Isaiah makes the same point:

He will swallow up death in victory; and the Lord God will wipe away tears from off all faces; and the rebuke of his people shall he take away from off all the earth: for the Lord hath spoken it. (Isaiah 25:8)

Hallelujah! JESUS IS THE LORD.

Chapter Eleven

THE BELIEVERS' DAILY PRAYER CONFESSION

In order to appreciate who we are in Christ, we need to personalise Ephesians 1:16-23 and pray it daily:

[I] cease not to give thanks for you, making mention of you in my prayers; that the God of our Lord Jesus Christ, the Father of glory, may give unto you the spirit of wisdom and revelation in the knowledge of him: the eyes of your understanding being enlightened; that ye may know what is the hope of his calling, and what the riches of the glory of his inheritance in the saints, and what is the exceeding greatness of his power to us-ward who believe,

according to the working of his mighty power, which he wrought in Christ, when he raised him from the dead, and set him at his own right hand in the heavenly places, far above all principality, and power, and might, and dominion, and every name that is named, not only in this world, but also in that which is to come: and hath put all things under his feet, and gave him to be the head over all things to the church, Which is his body, the fullness of him that filleth all in all.

Chapter Twelve

THE THREE MAJOR REALMS OF A BELIEVER'S OPERATION

Believers should understand this fundamental truth about the scope of operations of resurrection power. Every blood-bought, Bible-believing and Holy Ghost-filled believer has been given power to exercise dominion authority in three major realms: we are seated together in heavenly places with Christ as kings and priests, reigning and ruling as we operate authoritatively in **the heavens**, on **the earth** and **beneath the earth.** According to Philippians 2:8-10:

And being found in fashion as a man, he humbled himself, and became obedient unto death, even the death of the cross. Wherefore God also hath highly exalted him, and given him a name which is above every name: That at the name of Jesus every knee should bow, of things in heaven, and things in earth, and things under the earth.

The death and resurrection of our Lord Jesus Christ brought everything under His feet. Thus it was resurrection power which brought about deliverance, restoration and reconciliation of all things back to the church (the Body of Christ):

Who hath delivered us from the power of darkness, and hath translated us into the kingdom of his dear Son: in whom we have redemption through his blood, even the forgiveness of sins: who is the image of the invisible God, the firstborn of every creature: for by him were all things created, that are in heaven, and that are in earth, visible and invisible, whether they be thrones, or dominions, or principalities, or powers: all things were created by him, and for him: and he is before all things, and by him all things consist. And he is the head of the body, the church: who is the beginning, the firstborn from the dead; that in all things he might have the preeminence. For it pleased the Father that in him should all fulness dwell; and, having made peace through the blood of his cross, by him to reconcile all things unto himself; by

him, I say, whether they be things in earth, or things in heaven. And you, that were sometime alienated and enemies in your mind by wicked works, yet now hath he reconciled in the body of his flesh through death, to present you holy and unblameable and unreproveable in his sight: if ye continue in the faith grounded and settled, and be not moved away from the hope of the gospel, which ye have heard, and which was preached to every creature which is under heaven; whereof I Paul am made a minister. (Colossians 1:13-21)

SPECIAL PRAYER AND BENEDICTION

Now may the God of peace [the source of serenity and spiritual well-being] who brought up from the dead our Lord Jesus, the great Shepherd of the sheep, through the blood that sealed and ratified the eternal covenant, equip you with every good thing to carry out His will and strengthen you [making you complete and perfect as you ought to be], accomplishing in us that which is pleasing in His sight, through Jesus Christ, to whom be the glory forever and ever. Amen. (Hebrews 13:20-21).

It is my prayer that God will give you understanding and revelation about the immeasurable power of resurrection as made available to us through Jesus Christ. Amen!

SHALOM! SHALOM! SHALOM!